LIFE THEREIN

A MOMENT AT A TIME

MATTHEW D. HUNT

MATTHEW D. HUNT

Printed in the United States of America

First Printing, 2023

Library of Congress Control Number: 2023905379

Paperback ISBN# 979-8-9880228-0-0

Hardback ISBN# 979-8-9880228-1-7

Ebook ISBN# 979-8-9880228-2-4

www.mdhuntbooks.com

For Piper, Alexander, and Cameron,

My loves, my life, my legacy,

This book is yours to keep forever,

The best of me, my heart's endeavor.

So take this book, hold it tight,

May it inspire and bring you light,

And know that in each page you'll see

A piece of me for eternity.

ACKNOWLEDGMEN

For my friends Joe Ochman & Ellen Dubin: Thanks for the encouragement, for always kicking me back into play and never failing to make me laugh with your goofy phone calls.

Amidst this fleeting life, I feel obliged

To recognize friends who've stood by my side,

Cheering me on through thick and thin

And offering wisdom as if they were kin.

Your friendship means the world to me,

And I just wanted to take this chance to say,

Thank you for always being there,

And for brightening up my day.

CONTENTS

CHAPTER ONE

AN AUTHOR'S PERSPECTIVE

Failure

Failure, oh failure, my old pal,

You always seem to make me take a fall.

I try my best, I give my all,

But it seems my efforts are quite small.

My plans have gone completely awry,

And now all I can do is sit and sigh.

But what's the use of crying now?

I just have to figure out how.

Failure, oh failure, my old friend,

You visit me time and again,

No matter how hard I may try,

I always seem to catch your eye.

I thought I had it all figured out,

Success was just a matter of doubt,

But then you came and showed me the way

Straight to the land of dismay.

Failed at diets and failed at dreams,

Failed at even the simplest of schemes.

But as I sit here with my frown,

I can't help but laugh at being the clown

That I've become in the face of defeat,

The one who trips over his own two feet.

So bring on the failure, I say,

Let it come and have its way,

For in the end, I'll still be here,

Laughing at my own despair.

And maybe one day I'll succeed,

But until then, I'll never concede.

I thought I had it in the bag,

But instead I'm left with this sad rag.

Failure is my old friend,

And it's a relationship that won't end.

Lost In Words

Language flows like a river.

My thoughts they twist and quiver.

I try to find my way, a guide,

But the words they won't subside.

Sentences stretch on for miles,

Paragraphs build up in piles,

I'm lost in the depths of my mind,

A maze of words hard to unwind.

Each word a puzzle piece to find,

Playing hide-and-seek inside my mind.

I'm searching for meaning, for truth,

But the words, they just won't come forth.

Lost in words, a place of wonder,

A never-ending cosmic thunder.

Words swirl around me, a dizzying haze

Of letters and phrases in bewildering craze.

I'm lost in their midst with no end in sight,

A world of language, a blinding light,

Each word a brushstroke, a stroke of the pen,

A picture painted, a story begun.

I'm lost in the colors, the rhythm and rhyme,

A symphony of words, a dance in time.

I'm caught in their spell, a captive of verse,

A prisoner of language, a blessing and curse.

Yet amidst the confusion a clarity shines,

A message emerges, a truth that aligns.

The words become clear, a beacon of light,

And I find my way through the endless night.

With each step the journey unfolds,

A tale to tell, a story to be told.

In the end I find my way,

The words finally have their say.

CHAPTER TWO

RAISING CHILDREN

My Princess

Once upon a time in a land far away,

A little girl in a princess dress came to play.

With a twirl and a spin, she looked like a dream,

But she was on a mission, or so it did seem.

For you see, she was a warrior princess, so bold,

And she needed her battle axe, to be brave and hold,

She searched high and low, through every nook with a bound,

But her axe was nowhere to be found.

With a stamp of her foot and a pout on her face,

She searched some more at a faster pace,

She checked under the bed and in the closet too,

But no axe in sight, what was she to do?

She asked her dad, who just chuckled and grinned,

"Your battle axe, my dear, is found within,"

And with a laugh and a hug, he sent her on her way,

To play and have fun, on this sunny day.

So the little girl twirled and spun, with glee in her heart,

Her princess dress aflutter, like a work of art,

For in her mind, she was still a warrior princess bold,

Even without a battle axe in hand, she was still worth her weight in gold.

First Moment

The moment you hold your child in your arms,

You're filled with a love that's pure and warm.

A love that brings joy beyond measure,

And fills your heart with endless treasure.

But as you look into their eyes so bright,

You also feel a fear take flight.

A fear of all the things that could go wrong,

Of the challenges that lie ahead so long.

You worry about their health and their dreams,

About their struggles and their screams.

You worry about the world they'll face,

And the pain they'll feel in every race.

But even in the midst of all your fears,

You know that love will conquer all your tears.

You know that you'll be there through thick and thin,

With all the love and support that's within.

For being a parent is a journey of joy and fear,

A path that's not always perfectly clear.

But with each step you take, you'll grow

And learn to love more deeply than you ever know.

So let your heart be filled with love and light,

As you guide your child through every fight.

For the joy and fear of being a parent,

Is a journey worth taking, every moment.

A Father's Love

A father's love for his children, a bond beyond compare,

A love so strong, it's felt everywhere.

The joy, the fear, the hope, all intertwined

As he embarks on this journey, with love in his mind.

He holds his children, so fragile and small,

Wondering how he can protect them from it all.

He fears for their future, what it may hold

But knows he'll be there, as they grow old.

With each passing day he watches them grow,

Teaching them, guiding them, as they learn and know,

The wonder and awe of seeing them succeed

Brings tears to his eyes and fills him with pride, indeed.

He marvels at their innocence, their laughter, and their smile,

The way they see the world makes it all worth the while.

And in their eyes, he sees the reflection of his soul

And knows that his love for them will always be whole.

As they grow older and venture out on their own,

He watches them soar, their independence shown,

But his love for them never fades, it only grows,

As they find their way and make their own shows.

A father's love for his children, a bond beyond compare,

A love so strong, it's felt everywhere.

The joy, the fear, the hope, all intertwined

As he embarks on this journey, with love in his mind.

A Path Begun

A new life has just begun,

A tiny spark of hope and fun,

Infinite possibilities ahead,

A bright future waiting to be led.

This newborn child, pure and new,

Has the world at their feet, it's true.

What will they become, where will they go?

Only time will tell, but one thing we know,

Their potential is boundless, their talents unique,

A future full of promise, they are destined to seek,

With each passing day, they will grow and learn,

From their mistakes they will rise and turn.

Their dreams will become their reality,

Their determination will lead to prosperity,

No mountain too high, no challenge too great,

They'll conquer all and fulfill their fate.

As they grow, they'll find their way,

Discovering their passions day by day,

And with every step, they'll create their destiny,

Leaving their mark on history.

So let us celebrate this new life,

Full of hope, joy, and possibility rife,

For this newborn child has so much to give,

A shining star in this world, ready to live.

Possibility

I look into their eyes and what do I see?

The future, the destiny, the possibilities.

There's a glimmer of hope, a spark of ambition,

A dream in their heart, a vision of fruition.

I see a path ahead, winding and wide,

Full of challenges, but they won't hide.

For they have the strength, the courage, the will

To forge ahead, to climb every hill.

The future is theirs, and they know it well.

They'll make their mark, they'll break every spell,

They'll leave a legacy, a lasting impression,

A trailblazer, a pioneer, an inspiration.

I see the future in their eyes, bright and clear,

A world of opportunities, of joy and cheer.

And I know that they'll make it, they'll soar high

For they have the future in their eye.

Coming Out

A moment of truth, a moment of fear,

A child coming out to a parent dear.

Heart beating fast, palms sweaty and cold,

Wondering if love will still unfold.

The words are heavy, yet they must be said,

For the truth within cannot be unread.

A parent's love, so pure and strong,

Will it remain, or will it be gone?

The child takes a breath, and speaks with care,

And the parent listens, with love to share.

The fear subsides as the love pours out,

And the child knows without a doubt.

That love knows no bounds, no race or gender,

And a parent's love, will always render

A safe haven, for a child's heart to rest

With love and acceptance, that's truly the best.

For the child who's come out, it's a start anew,

Living life honestly, and being true.

With support and love from those who care,

They can live life fully, without a fear to bear.

So let love prevail, let it guide the way,

And let acceptance be the light of the day.

For when a child comes out to a parent's embrace,

It's a beautiful moment, full of love and grace.

Dad

Being a dad is quite a thing,

Full of surprises and endless bling,

From being a jungle gym to a hero in a cape,

Even if you're out of shape.

Being a dad is a wild ride,

Full of laughter, tears, and pride,

From changing diapers to playing catch,

It's a journey that's hard to match.

The kids will test your patience, that's for sure,

But the joy they bring is an endless lure,

From scraped knees to sassy mouths,

It's all part of the parenting bouts.

You'll hear "Daddy, can I have a pony?"

And "Daddy, can you make macaroni?",

You'll even hear "Daddy, can you fix my hair?"

And somehow, you'll become a stylist with no compare.

The sleepless nights and early mornings,

Will make you feel like you're just performing,

But when they say "I love you, Dad",

All those troubles don't seem so bad.

Being a dad is a crazy ride,

Full of love, laughter, and sometimes, surprise,

But in the end, it's worth the strife

To be a part of your child's life.

Light

A daughter's smile, a ray of sunshine in a father's life,

A moment of pure joy, free from any strife,

It lights up the room and warms his heart,

Bringing him hope and love, never to depart.

He watches her grow, her smile evolves

From a tiny grin, to a full smile so bold.

And though time may pass, life may change,

Her smile remains a constant that's never estranged.

He treasures every moment where her smile shines so bright,

And cherishes the memories that come with such delight.

For her smile is a reflection of her heart so true,

And he's grateful for each moment spent with his daughter too.

He knows that life may not always be so fair,

And that challenges and struggles will be there,

But her smile gives him hope and the strength to persevere,

To keep going no matter what he may fear.

A daughter's smile, a ray of sunshine in a father's life,

A moment of pure joy, free from any strife.

It reminds him of the love that's always there,

And fills him with hope and the courage to dare.

My Son

A father's hope for his son, an unwavering dream,

A hope that's filled with love, and a future that gleams,

He watches him grow, with pride and with care.

Guiding him along the way, with wisdom to share,

He hopes that his son will grow up to be kind,

With a heart full of love and an open mind.

That he'll be brave and strong, with a spirit so free,

And that he'll find his passion, whatever it may be.

He hopes that he'll be honest, always do what's right,

With integrity and honor, shining bright.

That he'll stand up for what he believes, with courage and might

And make a difference in the world, with his inner light.

Rise Up

A father's fear for his children, a weight he can't ignore,

For every single day, his love grows more and more.

The fear of what they'll face as they journey through life,

The thought of all the struggles that may cut like a knife.

He fears for their hearts, and the trials that may come,

For the moments that may break them, and leave them feeling numb,

He fears for their dreams, and the paths they'll pursue,

And whether they'll find happiness to last them through and through.

He fears for their safety, in a world not so kind,

With dangers lurking everywhere, and peace hard to find,

He fears for their minds, the things they may be told,

The pressures they may face, and the lies they may behold.

But amidst all of his fears, he holds onto his hope,

That his children will rise up, and find strength to cope,

That they'll face every challenge with courage and grace,

And they'll find their way through life, at their own steady pace.

He'll be there to guide them and support them every day,

To offer his love and wisdom every step of the way.

For a father's fear for his children may seem hard to bear,

But with love, hope, and faith, he'll help them find their way with care.

Masculinity

My dear son, I want you to know

that masculinity is not a show

of bravado or forceful might,

It's about being just, and doing what's right.

Some might say that to be a man

Is to be tough and take a stand,

To be a bully, to push and shove,

But that's not the way to show your love.

True masculinity is something more.

It's about caring, and what you stand for,

It's about being strong in body and mind,

And helping those in need, you'll find.

To be a man is to defend

The weak and vulnerable, my friend.

To be a man is to be kind,

To show empathy and compassion in your mind,

To treat others with respect and care,

To lend a hand, to always be there.

It's about treating others with kindness and respect,

And never letting your ego take control and deflect.

Your true nature as a caring soul,

Who will always lend a helping hand, to make others whole.

This is what it means to be a man,

And how to live your life as best you can.

So, my son, remember this well,

True masculinity is a story to tell.

It's not about being a bully, or pushing your way,

It's being strong, yet kind and caring, every day.

Fly, My Love

As I watch my child grow up and leave,

My heart breaks in two, I can hardly breathe.

For so long, I held them close, kept them near,

But now they're ready to face their fear.

The fear of the unknown, of what lies ahead,

As they take that step, I feel so much dread,

For they are my child, my flesh and blood,

And the thought of them being alone makes my heart flood.

I remember the first time they cried,

The sleepless nights I spent by their side,

And now, as they leave, my heart aches

For the bond we shared, it now breaks.

I know they must spread their wings and fly,

But I can't help but feel I'll never say goodbye,

For even as they venture out on their own,

My love for them will never be outgrown.

So go, my child, and chase your dreams,

No matter how impossible they may seem,

But know that I'll always be here,

To guide you through your joy and fear.

CHAPTER THREE

INSPIRATION

Spirit

When disappointment and fear come to call,

And your dreams seem to crumble and fall,

It's easy to feel lost in the dark

As hope fades and leaves its mark.

But remember, my dear, that within you lies

The strength to overcome and rise,

To face the challenges that come your way.

Seize the opportunity to make a brighter day.

The path may be rocky and steep,

But with each step your courage will leap,

Though fear may try to hold you back,

Your determination will keep you on track.

Take a deep breath and gather your might,

And let your spirit shine bright,

For in the face of disappointment and fear,

You have the power to persevere.

Believe in yourself and all you can achieve,

With each obstacle, you will believe

That nothing can stop you or hold you down,

For you are strong, brave, and profound.

Hold your head high and keep moving ahead,

And remember, my dear, that you are not alone or dead,

For with each challenge, you grow and learn,

And your spirit will continue to burn.

Undiscovered

I wander through this crowded place,

A sea of faces lost in the race,

And though I long for company,

It seems no one notices me.

I smile and wave, but no one looks,

My heart sinks as I turn and book,

Another day of solitude,

A life in which I feel excluded.

It's hard to bear this sense of lack,

To feel ignored, and pushed to the back,

To watch as others form connections

While I am left with my reflections.

But deep within, I know it's true

That I am worthy, and deserving too,

Of love and kindness, friendship and care,

Of all the things that make life fair.

So though it hurts to be passed by,

I'll keep my head held high,

And trust that someday, somehow,

I'll find my place, my time, my now.

For in this world of endless chance,

There's always hope, a new romance,

A friend to meet, a bond to form,

A life that's waiting to be born.

I Am Me

I wake up each day with a heart full of joy,

No need for approval, or to play coy,

For I am happy with myself, just as I am,

Unique and imperfect, yet still a true gem.

I don't compare myself to those around,

For I am me, and that's where my happiness is found.

I celebrate my strengths, embrace my flaws,

For they make me human, and open up new doors.

I find pleasure in simple things,

A quiet moment, or a bird that sings,

I don't need much to feel content,

Just a heart full of love, and a mind that's present.

I won't let others bring me down,

Or make me feel like I'm just a clown,

For I am happy with who I am,

And that's all that matters, in the end.

I Am Not My Disability

Of all the things I wish to be,

Not one of them is a disability.

But life can have its twists and turns,

And fate can give us lessons to learn.

So here I am, in a different lane,

Navigating challenges with grit and brain.

My body may falter, but my spirit is strong,

And I will never let my dreams go wrong.

Some may pity, some may judge,

But I will not begrudge.

I am a person with passions and goals to unfold,

A heart that beats, and a story to be told.

So look beyond the surface view

And see the person that's shining through.

With kindness, empathy, and an open mind,

We can leave our limitations behind.

Life is a journey with ups and downs,

And we all deserve to wear the crowns.

So let us hold fast, hand in hand,

And create a world that we all can understand.

Persevere

When life knocks us down and we feel so small,

When everything seems to crumble and fall,

We must remember to persevere and rise,

For even in darkness hope never dies.

We may stumble and falter along the way,

But with each step forward we're stronger, we're okay.

We gather our strength and we stand up tall,

Ready to face the challenge, to give our all.

We take a deep breath, we start anew

With a clear focus and a goal in view.

We learn from our mistakes and we grow so wise,

For even in failure, there's always a prize.

It's not about perfection or getting it right,

It's about the journey and the fight.

The strength we gain from each and every try,

And the lessons we learn as we reach for the sky.

So when life throws us a curve and we feel so low,

We must remember to never let go.

To keep on going, and to persevere,

For the joy of starting over, it's always near.

With each new day, we have a chance,

To make a difference, to take a stance.

To live our dreams, and to reach so high,

For the power of perseverance, it never dies.

So let us stand strong, and let us begin,

With a fire in our heart, and a determined grin.

For when we persevere, and we start anew,

The possibilities are endless, and the future's bright and true.

Live

In life, we sometimes hesitate

To try something new, to take the bait.

We fear the unknown and the chance we'll fail,

So we stick to what's safe, and miss the sail.

But as we age, and we gain more grace,

We realize it's never too late to chase.

To chase our dreams and take a leap,

To try something new and break the keep.

For though we may be older and our bones may creak,

We still have the power to seek and peak,

To learn a new skill or take on a new role,

And fill our hearts with a brand new goal.

We may stumble and fall as we try to find our way,

With each step we take, we'll grow more confident without dismay.

We'll find a sense of purpose and a renewed sense of hope,

As we embrace the unknown, and the endless scope.

For trying something new later in life

Can be a beautiful thing, and lessen the strife.

It opens up doors we thought were long closed,

And can lead to adventures we never supposed.

So let us not be afraid to try something new,

For it may lead us to a life that's anew.

Let us embrace the unknown and take the chance

To live a life that's full and to dance the dance.

Be You

Be proud of your passion, let it ignite

A fire in your soul that burns bright.

Don't let others dictate your love and its way,

For theirs may differ from yours, and that's okay.

Follow your heart, let it be your guide,

And let your spirit soar with pride,

Don't be afraid to stand out from the crowd,

And let your passion speak out loud.

Respect the views of others as they do yours,

And never let their words close your doors,

For every journey is unique in its way,

And yours is no different, let it sway.

Believe in yourself and your abilities,

And don't let others limit your possibilities,

For passion is the fuel that drives us forward,

And it's what makes life truly explored.

So be proud of your passion, embrace it tight,

And let it lead you to the height

Of your dreams and aspirations,

And a life filled with celebrations.

You Are Worthy

There will always be someone who can't see,

The value that lies within thee,

Do not let that someone be you,

For you are worthy, through and through.

The world may not judge you by your worth,

And seek to bring you down to earth,

But don't let their opinions define

The light that within you shines.

Believe in yourself and your potential,

For you are capable and essential,

Don't let the naysayers get you down,

And wear your worthiness like a crown.

You are unique, with gifts to share,

And no one can take that from you, so beware

Of the doubt and fear that may arise,

And remember to look within, and realize

That you are worthy, no matter what they say,

And your worth will shine brighter each passing day,

So don't let anyone dim your light,

Or let your worthiness take flight.

For there will always be someone that does not see,

The worth that lies within thee,

But let it not be you, my friend,

For your worthiness has no end.

Fear

An ominous shadow looms ahead,

As I traverse this path with dread,

The fear of failure grips my heart

And tears my confidence apart.

What if my efforts are all in vain,

And I am left with naught but pain?

I know I must take this chance

To reach for greatness and advance,

Yet thought of failure is a weight

That makes me hesitate.

I know I cannot let it win,

This fear that whispers from within,

For only by taking risks can I

Reach the heights that make me fly.

I take a deep breath and try

To silence the doubts and deny,

Though the journey may be tough

And failures may be part of the rough.

I will push through and persevere,

Fear of failure won't interfere.

The fear of failure, oh how it grips,

A monster that sneaks in and strips

Confidence and courage, leaving behind

Anxiety and doubt, clouding the mind.

A daunting challenge lies ahead,

A dream to chase, a path to tread,

The thought of stumbling and falling flat,

Of facing judgment and harsh critique,

Can make the bravest soul feel weak.

But failure is not the end, we know,

It's just a setback, a chance to grow,

So let us not be held by fear,

Let it not stop us here,

For success is not just winning,

But also about getting up and beginning.

Let us embrace the fear of failure,

And use it to push ourselves higher,

To chase our dreams, to reach new heights,

And to let our courage take flight.

I have the courage to face my fears,

To rise above the doubts and tears.

Endeavor

The journey begins with a single step,

A new endeavor, with risks to accept.

The road ahead is long and unknown,

But the possibilities are waiting to be shown.

Excitement and fear, a mix of emotion,

As the heart beats with newfound devotion.

The fire within, burning bright and strong,

Ready to push forward and carry on.

The dream is alive, the passion so real,

A new endeavor, with so much to reveal.

The mind races with plans to create,

And the spirit soars with no time to wait.

Obstacles may come, but they won't deter,

For the strength within is the great nurturer.

Determination fuels the fire to burn,

And the will to succeed is the great return.

With each step forward, the path becomes clear,

And the goal is within reach, so very near.

The heart overflows with joy and pride,

As the new endeavor takes a great stride.

And so the journey continues, with purpose and drive,

A new endeavor, with endless possibilities to thrive.

With faith and courage, the sky is the limit,

And the success that comes is truly magnificent.

Give It Time

There's a common notion in our society

That success must come in youth's prime,

But I've learned through life's adversity

That success can come at any time.

I've chased my dreams with all my might,

Through struggles, hardships, and strife,

And though the road was long and tight,

I found success later in life.

It's not a race to the finish line,

Nor is it about beating the clock,

It's about persevering through decline,

And never giving up on your stock.

For every moment, every breath we take,

Is another chance to rise,

And every mistake we make

Is an opportunity in disguise.

So don't be discouraged by age or time,

Or by the failures of yesterday,

For every day is a fresh climb

To find success in our own way.

And when success comes, whenever it may be,

It's all the sweeter for the wait,

For the journey is what sets us free,

And success is the icing on the cake.

Believe In Yourself

When life is tough and doubts creep in,

And you feel like you just can't win,

Remember this, my friend, it's true,

The power lies within you.

You've got a strength that's all your own,

A light that shines, a heart that's grown,

With each challenge that you face,

You learn and grow, you find your place.

Don't listen to the voice of fear,

It'll try to stop you, make you veer

Away from all you know you're meant to be,

But trust me, friend, you've got what it takes to succeed.

Believe in yourself with all your heart,

And you'll find a way to make a start

On all the dreams you hold so dear,

And conquer any doubts or fear.

So take a deep breath and trust in you,

Believe in yourself, and all you can do,

For you're stronger than you realize,

And you've got what it takes to reach the skies.

You may feel lost, unsure of your worth,

But listen closely to these words:

You are capable of so much more

Than you've ever dared to explore.

Your dreams and passions may seem grand,

But don't let doubt and fear take command.

You have a unique set of skills and strengths,

And can accomplish great things at any length.

When obstacles block your path and way,

Believe in yourself and don't stray.

Remember that every challenge you face

Is an opportunity for growth and grace.

It's okay to stumble and fall,

But don't let those setbacks enthrall.

Dust yourself off, and stand up tall,

And keep pushing forward through it all.

So go ahead and chase your dreams,

No matter how big or small they seem.

Believe in yourself, and take that leap,

You'll realize all of the rewards you can reap.

Joy

In the midst of this bustling crowd,

I'm grateful for the energy, the sound,

For all the sights and smells and tastes,

For every moment that my heart races.

Though sometimes I may feel unhidden,

I know that my heart is full and unbidden,

Of opportunities to connect and grow,

To find new joys and let them flow.

I cherish the warmth of the sun on my face,

The laughter of children, their joy and grace,

The music that fills the air with sound,

The beauty of life that's always around.

And though my journey may be long,

I'm filled with hope, a new love song,

For every moment holds a chance,

To find true joy, to learn to dance.

So I'll keep my heart open wide,

To all the blessings that in me reside,

And know that life will bring me more,

Of all the things that I adore.

Chapter Four

HUMANITY

See Me

See me, not my disability,

Look beyond my physicality

And see the true essence of me,

My hopes, my dreams, my creativity.

I am more than what you see,

A spirit that longs to be free.

Don't let my disability define me,

It's only a small part of who I can be,

My heart is full of love and empathy,

A soul that craves to be set free.

Though I may move slower, or need some aid,

My dreams and aspirations will never fade,

I can achieve anything, I am not afraid

To challenge and break the barriers that were made.

My wheelchair may seem like a barrier,

But it's a vehicle that helps me get there,

To new destinations, new experiences to share,

To live life with purpose and flare.

My heart is big, my dreams are tall,

And I can accomplish them all.

I am not different, nor unique,

I'm full of abilities that are remarkable and chic.

My disability is not what defines me,

It's my strength, resilience, and tenacity.

Look beyond my disability

And you will see the true me,

A human being with a story,

A life that is full of glory.

Let's create a world where everyone is seen,

Where every person is valued and keen,

Where inclusion is not just in dreams

But is a reality that beams.

Together we can break the wall,

Build bridges, and create a world for all.

Stand Tall

Strive every day to stay on top of the H.I.L.L.,

With Honesty, Integrity, Loyalty, and Learning, fulfill,

No matter what you do or who you're with,

These values will help you stay true and be a gift.

Honesty is the foundation of trust,

In all relationships, it's a must,

Be truthful with yourself and others too,

And watch as honesty brings respect anew.

Integrity is doing the right thing

Even when no one is watching.

Stay true to your values and beliefs,

And watch as integrity brings relief.

Loyalty is a bond that's hard to break,

In good times and bad, it's a give and take,

Be loyal to those you love and trust,

And watch as loyalty brings abundance.

Learning is a lifelong journey of growth,

And it's something that's worth both,

Read, listen, and be open to new ideas,

And watch as learning brings endless frontiers.

So strive every day to stay on top of the H.I.L.L.,

With Honesty, Integrity, Loyalty, and Learning, fulfill,

No matter what you do or who you're with,

These values will help you stay true and be a gift.

Come Together

In the midst of gloom, a flicker of light,

A ray of hope, burning ever so bright,

Amidst the turmoil, the anguish, and the pain,

We can glimpse a path to a future sane.

For every predicament, there's a resolution,

For every challenge, a revolution,

For every sorrow, there's a healing,

For every conclusion, a fresh beginning.

We've seen the potency of love and solidarity,

The power in diversity and community.

We've witnessed the durability of the human soul

And the determination to surmount any goal.

We're capable of wonders and marvels,

Of shattering shackles, and tearing down walls,

The walls of hatred, bias, and fear,

And building a future that's equitable and clear.

So let's celebrate our distinctions and unite,

Let's preserve and nurture this planet in sight,

Let's envisage, envision, and innovate

A world that's righteous, impartial, and great.

The future is in our hands, it's up to us

To make it resplendent, gracious, and just.

Perfectly Different

The perfect day is hard to define,

It's different for me and different than thine.

For some, it may be sunny and bright,

For others, it may be a starry night.

But for me, the perfect day is one

Where the world is at peace, and love has won.

A day where the birds sing sweet melodies,

And the sun shines down on the greenest trees.

It's a day where I wake up with a smile,

And I know that everything is worthwhile.

I spend the morning in quiet reflection,

And meditate on the beauty of my connection.

Then I head out into the world with ease,

And feel the cool breeze rustling through the trees.

I meet friends old and new with an open heart,

And we share stories and laughter, a brand new start.

The afternoon is spent in peaceful bliss,

As I lose myself in a book or a movie's kiss.

And as the day draws to a close,

I watch the sunset with no woes.

The stars come out and twinkle bright,

And the moon shines down with all its might.

And as I drift off to sleep that night,

I thank the universe for this perfect day in sight.

Our Humanity

In humanity's heart, there lies great strength,

A power that transcends time and length.

A strength that fuels our will to survive,

And helps us overcome the toughest strife.

In times of darkness when all seems lost,

Humanity's kindness comes at a cost,

A cost that we're willing to pay

To help each other find a brighter day.

We've seen the strength of humanity's will.

When faced with challenges, we rise to the thrill.

Our capacity for love, for hope, for grace,

Shines through the darkness, and lights up the space.

We may stumble, we may fall,

But we rise again, standing tall,

For our strength comes from within

And we use it to heal and again begin.

So let us celebrate our humanity's strength,

Our guiding light to any length,

For with it we can achieve anything we dare,

And make this world a better place to share.

America

Oh America, land of the free

Our nation founded on ideals of unity

But lately we've allowed politics to divide

And forgotten what it means to stand side by side

We're all sisters and brothers, with the same dreams

To build a brighter future, or so it seems

But we let our differences tear us apart

And forget that we're all part of the same heart

We must come together, put aside our strife

And work towards a common goal, to improve our life

For the sake of our children, and future generations

Let's set aside our politics and build new foundations

And work towards a future of cooperation.

For we have the power to make a change,

And show the world our values remain,

So let's put aside our differences, and embrace our similarities,

And work together towards shared opportunities.

For America and all that we stand,

Let's unite and take each other's hand.

Differences

In this world, so vast and wide,

We are all on a different ride.

We come from different lands and homes,

But together we make beautiful poems.

Our differences, they may seem

Like a challenge or a dream.

But if we take a closer look

We'll find that they're what makes us unique.

Our skin, our culture, our language, our faith,

These are the things that make us great.

We should cherish them with all our might,

And celebrate them in full daylight.

For it is our differences that create

A tapestry that is woven in fate.

A symphony that is played with grace,

A rainbow that shines in all its space.

Let us embrace our diversity

And nurture it with all sincerity.

For in our differences we'll find

A world that's beautiful, and so divine.

Let us walk hand in hand,

And stand together, across this land.

For in our differences we'll see

A world that's rich and full of glee.

Actions

We abound in thoughts and prayers but we are dying from apathy
and avarice

Make Ends Meet

The daily grind of making ends meet,

Is a struggle that we all must greet.

We wake up early and work until late,

To put food on our plates and pay the rate.

Bills pile up, and debts accrue,

We wake up every morning,

The daily worries always anew.

With worries in our head,

How will we pay the bills

And keep our family fed?

We cut back on everything we can,

To keep up with the rising cost demand.

Our dreams and passions we put aside

In order to make a living and provide.

We sacrifice our time, and sometimes our health,

For the sake of financial wealth.

And sometimes we feel defeated,

But we must keep pushing forward,

For our dreams to be completed.

The struggle is real, the challenge immense,

But we must keep striving, and not lose our sense.

Let us not be defeated by the daily grind,

And the challenges that we often find.

Let us keep going, with our head held high,

And let our dreams take flight,

For with hard work and perseverance,

We'll make our future bright.

CHAPTER FIVE

LOVE AND FRIENDSHIP

That Moment

In one brief moment, my heart was caught,

A glance, a smile, a feeling sought.

A chance encounter, fate's decree,

That left its mark eternally.

In that one smile, a lifetime passed,

A future built, a die was cast.

A life together, yet to be,

A love so true, it seemed to me.

But as the crowd began to sway,

Your smile, your face, began to fade.

And though I searched both night and day,

My heart was left in disarray.

A lifetime lived, in one brief smile,

A love that lasted just awhile.

A moment cherished, but now gone,

A bittersweet memory, living on.

And though I may not see you now,

That moment stays, forever bound.

A life's worth lived in one short while,

For in that smile, my heart was found.

A Tapestry Woven

Memories are made of many things,

Of traits that stand out and make us sing.

Unique personalities, bright and bold,

Are etched in our minds and never grow old.

Shared interests that create a bond,

Bringing us closer, a friendship fond.

Life events that leave a lasting mark,

A wedding, a birth, a journey embarked.

Emotions that run deep, positive or not,

A connection that stays, never to be forgot.

Memories are made in so many ways,

Of the people we meet in our days.

A tapestry woven, a picture painted,

Of those who make life colorful and never faded.

L.I.G.H.T.

Love knows no gender

Inspirations know no age

Graciousness knows no race

Hope knows no social status

Thoughtfulness knows no judgement

Be someone's L.I.G.H.T.

Collaboration

Let not the envy of success

Diminish what you are,

For celebrating someone's triumphs

Will help you go far.

The world is not a battlefield

Where all must fight alone,

But rather a collaborative stage

Where all can feel at home.

The victories of another

Should not bring you despair,

But rather be a source of pride,

A reminder that you're there.

So let not the fear of loss

Stop you from lending a hand,

For helping others achieve their dreams

Will help you make a stand.

Be proud of those around you,

And celebrate their wins,

For together we can climb new heights,

And erase our doubts and sins.

Let not the fear of competition

Make life a zero-sum game,

For celebrating someone's success

Will make you feel the same.

Let us treat life as a collaboration,

And not a race to the end,

For together we can achieve so much,

And learn to be a friend.

True Friends

When the world feels too heavy to bear,

And the weight of it all is too much to wear,

There's a simple comfort that we can find

By being with someone who is kind.

Their presence alone can ease the ache

And make our troubles seem less opaque,

For in their company we find reprieve,

A respite from things we cannot leave.

In their embrace we find a calm,

And our worries soothed by kindness' balm.

Their warmth envelops us whole

And we feel less alone in our soul.

Their words may be few, but their meaning profound,

And in their silence, peace can be found,

For sometimes it's not what they say,

But the way they simply stay.

So let us cherish those who bring us ease

And be grateful for their presence;

Being with someone is comfort itself,

Their love and support is precious wealth.

CHAPTER SIX

PAIN AND GRIEF

Warrior

Behind a smile so bright and gay

Lies a pain that's hidden away,

A hurt that no one else can see,

A wound that won't let the heart be free.

In laughter, in joy, in all that's done,

The pain stays hidden, just for one,

A secret held close, never to share,

A burden too heavy, too much to bear.

The eyes may twinkle, the voice may ring,

But inside, a heartache still does cling,

A sorrow that eats at the soul,

A hurt that never lets one be whole.

Yet still the mask is kept in place,

A brave front shown to the human race,

For to let the pain be known

Is to risk the love that's grown.

And so, the pain stays hidden still,

A wound that won't ever fully heal,

But still, the smile remains intact,

A symbol of strength, a warrior's act.

Heart's Reaper

Pain and loss, a part of life,

The scars of which drive us toward strife.

When sorrow's waves come crashing down,

It's hard to keep our feet on ground.

In moments of heartache and despair,

It feels like no one else could care.

But in the midst of grief and pain,

We find we're not alone again.

Through tears we see the memories past,

The love we shared, a love that lasts.

Though our loved ones may be gone,

Their love and spirit lives on.

And though the pain may linger long,

We find that we can still be strong.

Through pain and loss, we learn to see

The beauty in life's fragility.

For in the wake of heartbreak's tide,

We find that hope will still abide.

The sun will rise, the night will end,

And we'll find joy in life again.

Passing

Pain and loss, they come to us all,

A bitter taste that we must recall.

In moments of heartache and despair,

It seems like life's too much to bear.

When a loved one passes or leaves our side,

Our world turns grey and we want to hide.

It's hard to find strength to carry on

When it feels like all our hope is gone.

But pain and loss can also teach

Lessons that are within our reach.

They remind us of life's fragility

And the need to love and show humility.

Though it may feel like a never-ending rain,

Time can heal and ease the pain.

And in the wake of grief and sorrow,

We can find new hope for tomorrow.

So don't lose faith in life's design,

For even in pain and loss, there's a sign.

A reminder of the love we've known

And the memories that will always be shown.

Hiding

Behind a smile I hide the pain,

A heart that hurts, again and again,

I put on a brave face every day,

And try to keep the hurt at bay.

I don't want anyone to see

The hurt and tears that consume me,

So I hide behind a mask of cheer

And pretend that nothing's wrong here.

But every night when I'm alone,

The pain comes back like a cyclone,

And I can't escape the hurt inside

No matter how hard I try to hide.

I wish I could let the pain out,

And scream and cry and shout,

But I'm afraid of what they'll say

And so I keep the pain at bay.

But maybe someday, I'll find the strength,

To let the pain out, at any length,

And show the world the real me,

Behind the mask of cheer they all see.

Until then I'll keep on smiling,

And keep the pain inside, beguiling,

For though I'm hurting deep within,

I'll keep the smile, and hope to win.

Heartbreak

Heartbreak and betrayal, they cut like a knife,

Leaving us shattered, wounded in life.

Our hearts are heavy, burdened with pain,

As we try to make sense of what we can't explain.

We wonder how it all went wrong,

As we try to find a way to move along.

The memories of love we shared before,

Now seem like they were nothing more.

Our hearts cry out for what we've lost,

As we try to navigate this new cost.

But as we grieve and start to heal,

We learn to see the truth that was concealed.

That love, though beautiful, is not immune

To the imperfections of the human commune.

We find the strength to forgive and let go,

As we learn to trust ourselves and grow.

We find new love, and it brings new light

As we move forward, no longer held in spite.

So let us remember when our hearts are sore,

That we can heal and love once more.

Though heartbreak and betrayal take their toll,

We are stronger and more resilient than we know.

We rise above the pain and strife,

And find happiness in a brand new life.

You Can Do This

In the midst of pain, it's hard to see

The light that shines beyond the agony.

But know that within you lies the power

To rise above the darkest hour.

Each step may feel like a mountain to climb

And tears may fall like raindrops in time,

But know that with every ounce of strength

You can push through the pain's great length.

Let hope be the anchor that holds you ready,

And faith be the compass that guides you steady.

Every trial that you endure

Will make you stronger, more resilient, for sure.

Take each day one step at a time,

And know that healing comes in its own time.

Don't give up, don't let go of the fight,

For the dawn comes after the darkest night.

And when you emerge on the other side,

Know that you have nothing to hide.

Your scars may be visible, but they bear witness

To the strength that lies within us.

For in overcoming pain, we find the key

To unlock the doors to the life we're meant to be.

So hold on tight, with all your might,

And know that in the end, everything will be all right.

Chapter Seven

CATS

The Rescue

A stray cat once roamed the streets,

A lonely soul with no retreat.

She searched for scraps and shelter too,

A life so hard, she barely knew.

Her fur was matted, her eyes so sad,

No one to love her, no one to be her dad.

She braved the cold, the summer heat,

Hoping for a home, a warm retreat.

Then one day a kind soul came by

And saw the beauty in her weary eyes.

He took her in and gave her love,

A forever home sent from above.

The cat now lounges in her cozy bed,

Her belly full, her fur so well-fed.

She has toys to play with, a family too,

A life so sweet, a dream come true.

She purrs and cuddles with her new friends,

Her heart so full, her joy never ends.

She knows that she's found her forever home,

And she'll never again have to roam.

The stray cat has now found her place,

A life so full of love and grace.

And though she'll never forget her past,

She's found her happiness at last.

Ruler

I am but a feline, small and sleek,

With eyes that gleam and fur so chic.

I roam around my home with ease,

Basking in the love that's given to me.

My humans shower me with affection,

Petting my head and rubbing my midsection.

I stretch and purr, my heart so full,

Knowing that I am loved, it's beautiful.

They play with me and give me treats,

And when I'm naughty, they don't skip a beat.

They scold me gently and then forgive,

Their love so strong, it's the only way to live.

I cuddle close and hear their hearts beat,

A rhythm so soothing, it's oh so sweet.

Their arms around me, their warmth so true,

I know that they'll always see me through.

For though I am but a tiny cat,

My humans love me, it's a simple fact.

And as I drift off to sleep tonight,

I'll dream of love, so pure and bright.

Human Pets

Cats. The rulers of the house,

So aloof, so sneaky, like a stealthy mouse.

With fur so soft and eyes so bright,

They can make us humans do whatever they like.

They sleep all day and party all night,

Leaving us to clean up their litter box plight.

They scratch our furniture, our curtains, and more,

And yet we still adore them, even when we're sore.

Their purrs and meows, their demanding cries,

Make us jump to their every guise.

They want food, they want toys, they want attention too,

And they'll make us work for it, oh yes they do.

But let's not forget, their antics are hilarious,

Like when they chase their tails or act so imperious.

They love to play and pounce on unsuspecting things,

And they'll do it all while wearing a pair of fluffy wings.

They curl up in our laps and make us smile,

Their warm bodies relaxing us for a while.

They bring us joy, they bring us peace,

Even if they shed their fur on our fleece.

So let's bow down to these regal creatures,

Who rule our homes with their cute little features.

For cats, oh cats, you're the real MVPs,

Thanks for bringing humor and love to our lives with ease.

Cats

Cats, you furry little fiends

With tails that swish and paws full of beans.

They nap all day and party at night,

Leaving us humans in sleepless plight!

They laze around without a care,

As if the world should simply share.

Their food, their toys, their cozy beds,

All belong to them, or so they've said.

Their purrs and meows, their demands so clear,

It's like they rule us, year after year.

They scratch our furniture, our favorite chair,

Yet we still adore them, we cannot bear.

For cats have a way with their charm,

They snuggle close, they cause no harm.

They curl up in our laps and purr,

And suddenly, all is right with the world, we concur.

Their curious nature, their playful glee,

Remind us to live life carefree.

To nap when we want, to play when we can,

And always remember to enjoy life's plan.

So let's raise a paw to these furry friends,

Who teach us to laugh and love till the end.

For cats, oh cats, you funny creatures,

Bring joy and laughter, and life's sweetest features.

Marks On My Heart

A whiskered face that I adored,

A playful soul that made me roar,

My furry friend, my feline mate,

Now lost, I mourn her untimely fate.

Her purrs once lulled me to sleep,

Her paws once danced around my feet,

But now her warmth no longer near,

I cry for her and shed a tear.

Her favorite toys lay still, unused,

No longer will she be amused,

Her bed now empty, blankets bare,

A void left by her absence, hard to bear.

Her memories, though, I'll always keep,

The way she purred and loved to sleep,

Her playful spirit, soft fur coat,

I'll hold onto tightly, and never let go.

My beloved cat, you'll always be

A cherished part of my memory,

Your love, your life, will never fade,

In my heart, your paw prints will be laid

CHAPTER EIGHT

NATURE

Nature's Beauty

Nature's beauty is a sight to behold,

A breathtaking canvas of colors and gold.

From towering mountains to crashing waves,

Its perfection leaves us all amazed.

But within nature's beauty flaws do lie,

A reminder of its imperfections nigh.

The raging storms and howling winds

Show the power that nature rescinds.

The lightning bolts that streak the sky

Are both perfect and flawed, as we ask why.

And though the rivers flow with grace,

Their strength can bring destruction in their embrace.

The trees that reach towards the sky

Sometimes fall and wither and die.

The flowers that bloom with hues so bright,

Fade and wilt, unable to fight.

Nature's perfection and flaws coexist,

A delicate balance that cannot be missed.

It's the flaws that make its beauty real,

A reminder of life's fragile and fleeting deal.

Nature's beauty and imperfections,

Are lessons in life's many reflections.

For with all its flaws and strife,

Nature is a perfect expression of life.

Earth

In this vast universe we call our home,

Our planet Earth is where we truly roam,

A precious gem amidst the void of space,

A place of beauty, wonder, and grace.

But as we thrive and multiply and grow,

We take and take and seldom give back, though,

Forgetting that we are but mere guests,

Takers of resources, and causes of unrest.

We've paved and polluted and destroyed

The very things that once brought us joy,

We've forgotten that we're part of the earth,

A symbiotic bond since before our birth.

We need the air, the water, the soil,

For us to live, to thrive, to uncoil,

We need the animals, the plants, the trees,

For us to coexist and find our peace.

It's time to awaken from our selfish dreams

And remember that the earth is more than it seems,

It's a living, breathing entity we're part of,

A cosmic dance we're invited to join and love.

Let's heal the earth and in turn, heal ourselves,

Let's take responsibility, and work for the commonwealth,

Let's nurture the earth and protect its precious life,

So that humanity can survive and continue to thrive.

Mountains

Towering high above the land,

The mountains stand majestic and grand.

A testament to nature's power,

They embody strength and endurance like a tower.

Their rugged faces, carved with time,

Bear witness to the elements and their prime.

The wind and rain, the sun and snow,

Have all left their marks and made them glow.

The mountains loom above the sky,

As if reaching out to touch the divine.

Their peaks shrouded in mist and cloud,

A mystical sight that leaves us wowed.

The trees and wildlife call them home,

Amidst the rocks and cliffs that they roam.

And as we journey through their might,

We feel their power, both day and night.

The mountains are a symbol of hope,

A beacon of light that helps us cope.

For though they may be rugged and steep,

Their beauty and grace always run deep.

The mountains teach us to persevere,

To climb higher and overcome our fears.

To be strong, resilient, and true,

Like the mountains that stand tall and new.

So let us gaze upon their grandeur,

And marvel at their wonder and splendor.

For the mountains are a gift to us all,

A reminder of life's majesty and call.

Chapter Nine

CHARACTER

Character

Judge a person by their character, not their skin,

Nor their beliefs, nor what they might win,

Not by their gender, nor their wealth,

For these are not the true measures of health.

A person's worth lies in who they are,

Not in their color or the scars they bear,

Not in the God they choose to pray,

Or the job they have to work each day.

Look into their heart, and you will find

The beauty that's within, so kind,

The love they share with those they know,

Their character is what makes them glow.

So judge a person by their worth,

And know that it's not about their birth,

Not about the color of their skin,

Or the religion they believe within.

If you judge someone by these things,

It's time to check your priorities and beliefs,

For a person's worth is not their gender or their race,

But in the content of their heart and their embrace.

Louder Than Words

Words may dance upon the tongue,

And lead the mind astray,

But actions speak a language true,

And show us who's at play.

For deeds reveal a person's heart

And motives hidden deep,

No matter what the words may say,

Their actions do not sleep.

If you seek to know someone,

And see beyond the guise,

Observe the things they choose to do,

And not just what they prize.

For words may charm and words may sway,

But actions do not lie,

They show us who a person is,

And what that may imply.

Thus, if you want to truly know

The truth behind the words,

Look at the actions of a soul,

And see what they've conferred.

Reality Check

Hold for me, in store so grand,

As I embarked on life's great plan.

But now I find that I am grown,

And all those dreams I once had sown

Have grown and changed, and some have died,

As life has taken me for a ride.

Responsibilities, they now abound,

And time seems scarce, it can't be found,

For work, for bills, for family too,

So much to do, so much to pursue.

And yet, I find that my dreams still accrue.

Don't Attack

When we're feeling insecure

And doubts begin to rise,

We may be tempted to demur

And criticize with unkind eyes.

But attacking others' work

Only leads to bitterness and strife,

It's like taking a dagger to the heart,

And shredding a precious life.

We all have different styles and skills,

And ways we choose to create,

To insult and tear down, only kills

The love and joy we should celebrate.

So let us lift each other up

And support each other's art,

For a kind and gentle word can create

A spark that kindles the heart.

And when we choose to spread goodwill

And praise the good we see,

Our own hearts will be filled

With a sense of generosity.

There's enough beauty to go around,

And enough room for every soul,

When we lift each other up, we've found

A place where love can take control.

Chapter Ten

HUMOR

Best Medicine

Humor is medicine, a cure-all for the soul,

A tonic for the weary, a balm for the whole.

It lightens the darkness, it chases away blues,

It adds a bit of sparkle to life's mundane hues.

It's a spark that ignites laughter, a twinkle in the eye,

A chuckle, a snicker, a guffaw, a sigh.

It's the punchline of a joke, the witty retort,

The playful banter, the clever report.

Humor breaks down barriers, brings people together,

Builds bridges, connects us, in fair or foul weather.

It's the great equalizer, it levels the playing field,

It cuts through pretensions, it makes us all yield.

So let us embrace humor, let us laugh and be merry,

Let us cherish the moments, let us not tarry.

For life is too short, too precious to waste,

Let us enjoy to the fullest, with humor and grace.

Nerd

I'm a sci-fi nerd, it's plain to see!

My favorite place the U.S.S. Enterprise, not in a tree.

I have a collection of lightsabers and phasers galore,

My favorite game is guessing which planet the Stargate will explore.

I dream of traveling through space and time

With the Doctor or with Jean-Luc, it would be sublime.

I'm a sci-fi nerd through and through,

My love for spaceships is nothing new.

From Star Wars to Star Trek, I've seen them all,

I know the difference between photon and phaser, big or small.

I dream of traveling the universe in a flash,

With a warp drive, a wormhole, or a hyperdrive dash.

Aliens, cyborgs, robots, and more,

I'm fascinated by what we'll find on some distant shore.

I've got a lightsaber replica by my bed,

And a Millennium Falcon model above my head.

I've read every book by Bradbury and Clarke,

And watched every episode of Doctor Who, it's a lark.

My friends don't get it. They say I'm bizarre,

But I just reply "Resistance is futile" like a Borg avatar.

I don't care if they think I'm out of my mind,

I'll keep watching my sci-fi shows and leave them behind.

So let the non-believers laugh and call me a dork,

I'll keep reading and watching, they can go to Ork.

I'm a sci-fi nerd, don't you know,

I love sci-fi more than pizza dough.

From alien invasions to robot wars,

My geeky heart beats for futuristic scores.

I dream of exploring the galaxy,

With a lightsaber or a sonic screwdriver, oh happily!

I've got a Starfleet uniform in my closet,

And a TARDIS replica, it's my coin deposit.

My friends they joke "Beam me up, Scotty",

But they don't get it, they're just being snotty.

I can quote Star Wars line by line,

And sing the Firefly theme, it's divine!

I know the difference between Star Trek and Star Gate,

And can explain a paradox without a single mistake.

I'll keep being a sci-fi nerd, with humor and glee,

Because who needs reality when there's a whole sci-fi galaxy?

Chores

Oh, house cleaning, how I dread thee!

The endless chores, the misery,

The dusting, the scrubbing, the vacuuming too,

It's enough to make me want to say "boo-hoo."

But alas, the mess won't clean itself,

The dishes won't magically find the shelf.

So I roll up my sleeves, and get to work,

Hoping the cleaning fairies won't shirk.

I start with the living room, oh what a sight,

Toys on the floor, and a pillow in flight.

I pick them up, and put them away,

And hope they'll stay, at least for a day.

Next comes the kitchen, where pots and pans

Are waiting to be washed and put back in their stands.

I scrub and I scour, and I wipe away,

And hope that I'll never have to do this again, any day.

The bathroom is next, the most dreaded of all,

With grime and germs, ready to make me fall,

I put on my gloves, my mask, and my hat,

And hope that I'll come out, still in one piece, at that.

And finally, the bedroom, where the laundry pile

Is waiting to be washed and folded, with a smile

I sort and I wash, and I hang them to dry

And hope that I won't hear a sigh.

But when it's all done, and the house is clean

I can sit down, and enjoy my caffeine.

Math

Mathematics is a tricky game,

A subject that fills me with shame,

No matter how hard I try,

My answers always seem to defy.

The numbers swirl around my head,

Multiplication, division, I'd rather be dead.

Fractions, decimals, what's the point?

All these calculations just make me want to leave this joint.

Geometry and trigonometry make me shiver,

Algebra, calculus, they make me quiver,

I can't remember the formulas no matter how I try,

I always seem to come up short, with a sigh.

My brain is wired for a different kind of art,

Mathematics to me, is like an alien part,

I'd rather write a poem or read a book

Or even be the cook.

So if you're looking for someone to solve a math equation,

You better look elsewhere, with no hesitation,

For I'm not the one, with a calculator I barely understand,

I'm just a funny poet, who counts on his hand.

I hope you've enjoyed these 60 poems.

"Wait... there are 63 of them!"

Oh, yeah... see above.

"Damn it Jim, I'm a writer, not a mathematician!"

ALSO BY

SOLAR REBOOT

When the solar flares first erupt, Cameron tries to rationalize the disaster away. The electrical grid will come back up. The government will reassure the panicked populace. The hurricanes, tornadoes, and earthquakes will abate. Most importantly, Cameron's husband and daughter will get home safely from New York City.

ABOUT THE AUTHOR

Born and raised in the Pacific Northwest, Matthew D. Hunt is a proud father of three, an award-winning author, and an Emmy-nominated filmmaker.

Throughout his career, Hunt has worked on a variety of T.V. series, short films, documentaries, and feature films. He has also written the multi-award-winning novel "Solar Reboot" which has been widely praised for its engaging characters, innovative world-building, and thought-provoking exploration of the human condition in a post-apocalyptic future.

In addition to his creative work, Hunt is also a dedicated teacher and mentor, having taught and lectured on writing and film at several conventions around the United States, including the honor of being a judge and lecturer for the Ms. Wheelchair USA competition for the past 5 years. His passion for storytelling and commitment to excellence continue to inspire others in the creative community.